Seven Wonders of
EXPLORATION
TECHNOLOGY

Fred Bortz

TWENTY-FIRST CENTURY BOOKS

Minneapolis

To future explorers—follow your questions!

Twenty-First Century Books
A division of Lerner Publishing Group, Inc.
241 First Avenue North
Minneapolis, MN 55401 U.S.A.

Website address: www.lernerbooks.com

Library of Congress Cataloging-in-Publication Data

Bortz, Alfred B.
    Seven wonders of exploration technology / by Fred Bortz.
        p.   cm. — (Seven wonders)
    Includes bibliographical references and index.
    ISBN 978–0–7613–4241–0 (lib. bdg. : alk. paper)
    1. Scientific apparatus and instruments—Juvenile literature. 2. Research—Juvenile literature. 3. Curiosities and wonders—Juvenile literature. I. Title.
    Q185.3.B68 2010
    500—dc22   2009017798

Manufactured in the United States of America
1 – DP – 12/15/09

Contents

1
2
3
4
5
6
7

INTRODUCTION

*P*EOPLE LOVE TO MAKE LISTS OF THE BIGGEST AND THE BEST. ALMOST TWENTY-FIVE HUNDRED YEARS AGO, A GREEK WRITER NAMED HERODOTUS MADE A LIST OF THE MOST AWESOME THINGS EVER BUILT BY PEOPLE. THE LIST INCLUDED BUILDINGS, STATUES, AND OTHER OBJECTS THAT WERE LARGE, WONDROUS, AND IMPRESSIVE. LATER, OTHER WRITERS ADDED NEW ITEMS TO THE LIST. WRITERS EVENTUALLY AGREED ON A FINAL LIST. IT WAS CALLED THE SEVEN WONDERS OF THE ANCIENT WORLD.

The list became so famous that people began imitating it. They made other lists of wonders. They listed the Seven Wonders of the Modern World and the Seven Wonders of the Middle Ages. People even made lists of undersea wonders.

People have always been explorers. Wherever they looked and whatever they saw, they wanted to discover more. Even as they explored all the wonderful lands of Earth and "the seven seas," they wanted to probe deeper, farther, and higher.

They invented vehicles to carry people and tools to the ocean depths, high into the atmosphere, or even to other worlds. They invented scientific instruments to explore the most distant parts of the universe and the smallest bits of matter (physical substances).

The list of wonders of exploration technology is very long indeed. Choosing "seven wonders" is not the same as choosing "*the* seven wonders." In selecting seven wonders for this book, we know that we are leaving out hundreds of other remarkable explorations that led us to amazing discoveries.

A Wonderful Adventure

Our seven examples display both the great questions that have led people to explore and the great technologies that have made those explorations possible. We begin on planet Earth, exploring the depths of the sea and the ever-changing atmosphere. Then, after our journeys carry us to the Moon and the planets, we explore the most distant reaches of the universe.

The discoveries we make there will lead us to many new questions and explorations. Those questions will carry us back to Earth, where we will visit a huge tunnel under the Alps. That is where scientists are using the world's most advanced technologies to probe the smallest particles of matter. Surprisingly, what they find in those particles may answer some of those cosmic questions, including how the universe began and how it became what it is today.

The Hubble Space Telescope photographed these two galaxies, part of a system of three galaxies that lie 400 million light-years from Earth. A light-year is the distance light travels in one year. In a year, light travels about 6 trillion miles (10 trillion km).

UNDERSEA Explorers

The undersea vehicle Alvin dives below the ocean waves on the way to the ocean floor 2.8 miles (4,500 meters) down.

OF ALL THE LARGE CREATURES ON EARTH, HUMANS ARE THE ONLY SPECIES THAT CAN BE FOUND ON EVERY CONTINENT. ALL OTHER PLANTS AND ANIMALS HAVE THEIR OWN NATURAL HABITATS. THEY THRIVE ONLY WHERE THE ENVIRONMENT PROVIDES EVERYTHING THEY NEED FOR LIVING—SUCH AS AIR, WATER, NOURISHMENT, AND SHELTER.

Our species first emerged in the grasslands of Africa. That area could still be called our natural habitat. But we have spread far beyond it. Unlike other animals, humans have the brains and bodies to create tools and technologies.

Starting with simple tools and fire, we found ways to survive in new places. Clothing and fire kept us warm in areas where the winter cold would otherwise kill us. Tools and weapons kept us safe from predators, and we became hunters instead of prey.

Early humans discovered or created things to make life easier, such as simple tools and ways to control fire.

The invention of scuba gear allowed people to breathe oxygen stored in tanks that they carried with them underwater. Divers could go deeper and stay underwater longer, opening up a whole new vision of what goes on below the seas.

We also became explorers, driven by the urge to discover. We can use modern technology to create a livable environment, at least for a few hours or days, almost anywhere on Earth—even in the ocean depths.

A WATERY WORLD

Oceans cover more than 70 percent of Earth's surface. We have explored every ocean and sea by boat and ship. We have learned about currents and water temperatures around the world. We have studied sea life by capturing it in nets and traps or by diving beneath the surface with air tanks on our backs.

But most of our knowledge about the ocean comes from near its surface. It is much harder to explore the deepest parts of the ocean. In some places, the ocean is deeper than the highest mountains are high. Very little sunlight reaches the depths. And anything we send deep in the ocean has to withstand the pressure of all the water above it.

How strong is that pressure? Let's compare it to air pressure. Air pressure comes from the weight of all the air above us. It pushes in every direction. It pushes so hard that it could squash our bodies flat. The reason it doesn't is that our bodies have hollow spaces. Those spaces are also filled with air. The air inside us is pushing out just as hard, balancing the pressure outside.

Water weighs much more than air. So water pressure is much greater than air pressure. At a little more than 30 feet (10 meters) below the ocean's surface, the water pressure is as great as the pressure of Earth's whole atmosphere. For every 30 feet farther down, the pressure increases by that same amount again. At a depth of about 2,400 feet (730 m), the water pressure is so high that it could crush a military submarine as easily as you could flatten a tin can with your foot.

As deep as that seems, most of the ocean is much deeper. Studying the deep ocean requires special vehicles and special equipment. These wonders of exploration technology are called deep submergence vehicles (DSVs, or submersibles) and remotely operated vehicles (ROVs).

DSVs and ROVs have produced amazing discoveries, but their work is just beginning. The oceans are so large and so deep that our greatest undersea exploring remains ahead of us.

This DSV, called Alvin, *carries a crew of a pilot and two scientists.* Alvin *can dive many times deeper beneath the ocean surface than the most advanced military submarines can go.*

UNDER THE OCEAN WITH ALVIN

What are the differences between a DSV and a submarine? Both carry crews underwater and have engines to move around. Both can be steered. Both need to be made of high-strength metals to withstand pressure. But most submarines are used for military purposes. Most DSVs are used for science and exploration.

Submarines carry crews of more than one hundred people. They can travel underwater at speeds higher than 30 knots. A knot is a nautical mile per hour—the equivalent of 1.15 miles (1.85 kilometers) per hour. Submarines can stay underwater for weeks or months at a time. They can also travel on the surface, at a slower speed.

A submersible is much smaller and slower. The most famous submersible is Alvin. The Woods Hole Oceanographic Institution in Massachusetts operates this DSV. Alvin has been exploring the ocean depths since 1964. It carries two passengers and a pilot to a depth of about 2.8 miles (4,500 m). That's more than six times as deep as the most advanced submarines. It dives so deep that it can reach 63 percent of the ocean floor.

Alvin must withstand the crushing water pressure at that depth. So the hull (protective outside) of its cabin has to be extra strong. Submarine hulls are made of high-strength steel, but that material is thick and heavy. Alvin needs something stronger yet more lightweight—titanium. Alvin's crew compartment is made of this metal.

A submarine is sleek and fast. But speed is not important to Alvin. It rides to the surface of its exploration site aboard a support ship called Atlantis. And once Alvin drops down to the ocean bottom, it doesn't need to travel very far.

This drawing shows a cross section of Alvin as it was designed in 1962. The crew space is the small, spherical room at left, in the front of the vehicle.

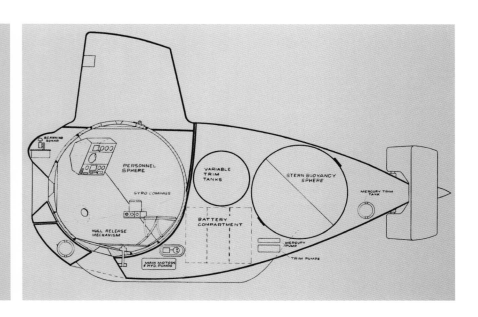

The two crew members prepare Alvin *for a dive. The* Atlantis, *seen at left, delivers* Alvin *to and from its diving locations.*

INSIDE *Alvin*

Exploring the sea bottom with *Alvin* is always exciting. But it is far from glamorous. A person taller than 5 feet 10 inches (1.7 m) can't stand up straight in *Alvin*'s crew compartment. And equipment for piloting or scientific tasks takes up most of the cabin space. At the ocean bottom, the water is about 35°F (2°C). *Alvin* has no heating system, so the inside temperature is only slightly warmer, thanks to heat from bodies and equipment. But no one complains about the chilly, cramped conditions when collecting scientific specimens and viewing undersea wonders through *Alvin*'s portholes.

The main cabin of *Alvin* is shaped like a sphere. That shape gives it the greatest strength with the least material. A submarine's engines and steering mechanism are inside the vessel. But *Alvin*'s are on the outside of its sphere. That's bad for speed, but it saves money by reducing the amount of costly titanium needed.

ROVs

Even with its money-saving design, exploring in *Alvin* is very expensive. And dangerous accidents are still possible. Why not use robots instead?

That is the idea behind ROVs. They are smaller and less expensive and have fewer limitations than DSVs.

Scientist Rhian Waller has explored the sea bottom using both. Waller is a deep-sea coral expert with the University of Hawaii. She says submersibles provide scientists a much better sense of the undersea world. "Nothing truly tells you the size of a large coral until you stare up at it from a submersible's porthole," she explains. "Actually turning left or right to get somewhere helps me find things at a later date, too."

But Waller notes that ROVs have advantages. *Alvin* carries only two observers and a pilot (the person who steers the craft). The craft is sometimes too large or too hard to steer where they want to go. And *Alvin* can only stay deep underwater for about eight hours before the crew needs to get back to *Atlantis*.

An ROV does not have any passengers. But more people can participate in the exploration. An ROV can send images to computers on its support ship—or to anywhere in the world. A group of people can look at the computer images as they arrive. An ROV can also stay undersea for days at a time. It doesn't have to worry about running out of air. It doesn't get tired or hungry. And it never needs to use a bathroom.

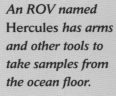

An ROV named Hercules has arms and other tools to take samples from the ocean floor.

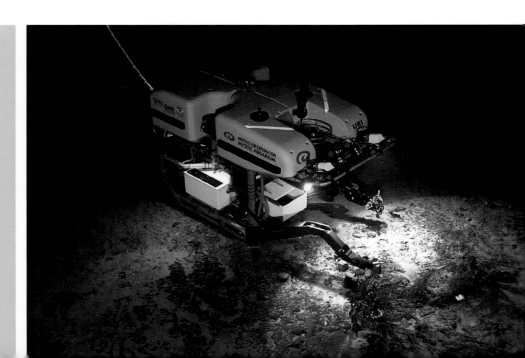

A hydrothermal vent known as a black smoker looks like an underwater chimney. Heated water and minerals from under Earth's crust flow out of these undersea vents. Alvin *helped scientists discover them.*

UNDERSEA DISCOVERIES

Alvin has taken part in many well-known undersea discoveries. In 1966 *Alvin* scientists found a dangerous bomb in the Mediterranean Sea near Spain. The bomb was dropped accidentally from a plane on a training mission. The recovery took more than two months and more than thirty-four dives in *Alvin*. When the bomb was first located and grabbed, it was lost again. It slipped away and slid down an underwater slope. *Alvin* found the bomb a second time, and it was successfully recovered.

In 1977 *Alvin* scientists explored deep under the Pacific Ocean near the Galápagos Islands. The islands are off the coast of South America. The scientists discovered something amazing on the seafloor. They found a spot where ocean water seeps into cracks in the ocean bottom. The water comes in contact with hot minerals deep inside Earth. The water heats up and flows out again, carrying some of the minerals with it.

"I remember the shimmering water coming from the vents and the unusual animals that humans had never seen before. . . . At the time it was all so weird and new."
—*Larry Shumaker, recalling the* Alvin *discovery of hydrothermal vents in 1977*

Scientists call the cracks hydrothermal vents. The heat and minerals make the vents an ideal home for bacteria and animal species. Scientists did not think that any creature could survive that deep in the cold ocean, where no sunlight reaches. But the Alvin team found bacteria, shrimp, clams, worms, and other life that humans had never seen before.

In 1986 *Alvin* took part in the discovery and exploration of the wreckage of the famous RMS *Titanic*. That passenger ship hit an iceberg and sank in the North Atlantic Ocean in 1912. *Alvin* carried a small ROV called *Jason Jr*. The ROV took photos and did detailed inspections of the Titanic wreckage in areas where *Alvin* could not go.

A New *Alvin*

In 2011 a newer model of *Alvin* will go into service. Its crew cabin will have more interior space (and headroom) and thicker, stronger titanium walls. It will be able to reach a depth of more than 4 miles (6,500 m). This will allow scientists to explore 99 percent of the ocean floor. Scientists such as Rhian Waller are anticipating amazing discoveries. But she is disappointed that one improvement hasn't been made. The new *Alvin* still won't have a bathroom.

This painting of the sunken Titanic *shows* Alvin *(below left) motoring around the bow in 1986. A year later,* Jason Jr. *took a photo (inset) of rows of dinner dishes that sunk with the giant ship.*

UNDERSEA *History Books*

Deep-sea corals are beautiful to look at. Coral reefs also have a scientific beauty. When the coral is alive, its skeleton grows. The number of living corals and the minerals in their skeletons change with the ocean conditions. Each year corals add a new growth band of coral skeletons to the reef. Each band gives information about the deep-ocean temperature and the nutrients that reached it from above.

Most undersea explorations don't attract the attention that those three events did. But *Alvin*'s work continues to be of great scientific importance. Rhian Waller's work with undersea corals is one example.

Corals are sea creatures that live in underwater colonies. Coral reefs are structures made of the skeletons of dead corals. Reefs build up over long periods of time. A close look at the reefs reveals bands similar to tree rings. The bands show how deep-sea conditions—especially the climate— changed over time periods as long as a quarter million years.

Waller is particularly interested in how corals adapt to such changes. Her work helps scientists understand how changing climates can affect the deep ocean. Dealing with climate change may be the most important issue for the world in the twenty-first century.

Rhian Waller holds up a piece of the deep-sea coral that she studies with the aid of Alvin.

2 EXPLORING *Earth's Climate*

Some parts of Earth (above) stay dry and hot year-round. Others (facing page) remain cold and covered with ice.

$\mathcal{H}$UMANS SHARE AN EXPERIENCE WITH BOTTOM-DWELLING SEA LIFE. WE TOO LIVE AT THE BOTTOM OF A DEEP GLOBAL OCEAN. BUT IT IS AN OCEAN OF AIR, NOT WATER. WE CALL IT THE ATMOSPHERE, AND WE COULD NOT SURVIVE WITHOUT IT.

That ocean of air is always changing. Some of its changes are quite predictable. We know that it is warmer in summer and colder in winter. We know it is warmer at the equator than near the poles. We know the air is thinner and colder in the high mountains than in lowlands. We know that some places on Earth are rainy, and others are dry. We know the seasonal patterns of the winds.

Those predictable patterns are what we call Earth's climate. Yet we all know that from day to day, the weather may be quite different from the usual climate. In late March, the weather is almost always hot and dry in Odessa, Texas. The region can go months without rain. But on March 30 and 31, 2000, it was cold and rainy. Did that mean the climate in Odessa had suddenly changed? No.

It was just a couple of days of rare rainy weather in the West Texas desert. But Earth's climate is changing in ways that concern people. For example, in the Arctic, the weather is much warmer than it used to be. The ice on Greenland may begin to melt and raise sea levels around the world.

How much and how fast will the seas rise? What other changes in climate lie ahead? Will rainfall patterns and growing seasons change? Will plants and animals (including humans) be able to adapt to a changed planet? Or will they be caught unprepared?

BUILDING A CLIMATE MODEL

To answer questions about Earth's climate, scientists go exploring. They make measurements on land, on sea, and up in the atmosphere. They measure the thickness of ancient tree rings to find clues to long-ago growing conditions. They drill deep into the polar ice, where the snow from every year is squeezed into thin layers. Some layers go back tens or hundreds of thousands of years! Since each layer traps bubbles of air from that year, the layers are like pages in an atmospheric history book.

A scientist removes an ice core drilled from the ice at Law Dome camp in East Antarctica. These scientists, known as glaciologists, learn about Earth's past climate changes by studying changes in polar ice.

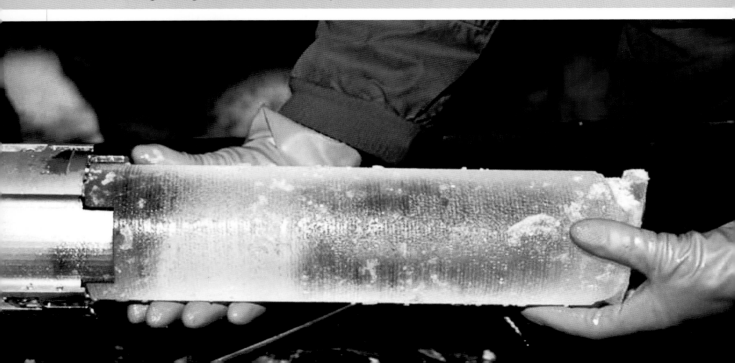

Computers help scientists study climate changes and track weather patterns.

WHAT IS A *Model?*

Scientists and engineers use the word *model* to describe a simplified but generally accurate version of a real thing. They can test things in the model that they can't change in reality. For instance, to model a giant volcanic eruption, they add a huge plume of dust and ash to the model's atmosphere. From that, they can calculate how the weather in North America might change several months later as dust and ash blow over the continent. Using historic records, they can evaluate the model's accuracy for such an event.

Weather explorers find clues in everything from fossils to old newspapers and weather records. And then they put all the evidence together to draw conclusions about how Earth's climate operates and changes.

Those measurements and clues tell us about the past climate. They tell us about detailed weather conditions in recent years and about newsworthy weather events in historical times. But most important, they help us build tools to predict what the weather and climate will be like in the future.

Those tools are computer programs. The programs begin with facts and figures called input data. A computer feeds input data into mathematical formulas and equations. The formulas and equations help scientists analyze all the data and draw conclusions from it.

Scientists call the programs climate models. Like a scale model of a bridge or building, a climate model is a simplified version of Earth's weather.

Scientists use climate models to study how Earth's weather changes as conditions in the atmosphere change. They can even make predictions about future changes. The programs need these facts and figures about Earth:

- A map of its landforms, oceans, lakes, and streams
- The energy reaching it from the Sun every second
- The gases in its atmosphere
- The tilt of its axis, which causes seasonal changes
- The length of a day and a year
- Weather or climate conditions at the start of the prediction period
- Other details that affect the prediction of future weather, such as dust or pollution in the atmosphere

The simplified climate model's predictions aren't always perfectly accurate. Still, the model can be tested with real data. After enough tests, scientists learn where its predictions are most useful. They also learn where it needs improvement.

Every model has limits. Even if its overall climate prediction may be accurate, no one expects the data to be right about every weather detail. Small changes in input sometimes produce large changes in predictions.

THE Butterfly Effect

Computer models have improved long-range weather forecasting. But predicting too far into the future usually produces useless results. Scientific measurements are never perfect, and a model never includes every detail about Earth. A small difference in input data in one place and time can have large effects on the model's predictions for other places in the world. This is sometimes called the butterfly effect. That term comes from mathematician and meteorologist Edward Norton Lorenz (1917–2008). Lorenz was not the first person to use the term, but he made it famous in 1979 when he presented a scientific talk about predictability. Its title asked, "Does the flap of a butterfly's wings in Brazil set off a tornado in Texas?" The title sounds like a joke. But Lorenz was making an important point. There is no way to account for every factor when trying to predict an event. Climate models can produce valuable knowledge. But we need to understand their limitations too.

"Climate is what you expect. Weather is what you get."
—*Robert A. Heinlein, science fiction writer, 1973*

USING CLIMATE MODELS

Besides predicting the current weather or climate, scientists use models to look at climate in the past. They use the models to explain historical climates and understand patterns. For example, geologists have found evidence that Earth's climate has cycled between ice ages and warm periods. Can a climate model explain that?

To model past climates, scientists need to use different input data. Astronomers know that Earth's orbit around the Sun slowly changes shape. Every one hundred thousand years or so, it cycles from more circular to more oval and back again. When the orbit is nearly circular, Earth gets about the same amount of sunlight every day.

When the orbit is more oval, the amount of sunlight varies. It is brightest and hottest when Earth reaches its closest point to the Sun. That point is called perihelion. And sunlight is least intense when the Earth is at its farthest point (aphelion).

Currently, Earth reaches perihelion on January 3. Over the next twenty-one thousand years, perihelion will gradually shift through the calendar until it returns to January.

If you live in the Northern Hemisphere, you may wonder how perihelion occurs in winter. If Earth is closer to the Sun, why is it so cold? But readers in Australia or Argentina might not ask that. In the Southern Hemisphere, January is midsummer.

No matter where you live, the answer is that seasons depend on something else—the tilt of Earth's axis. Each day, Earth spins around this imaginary line through its poles. In the northern winter, the North Pole is tilted slightly away

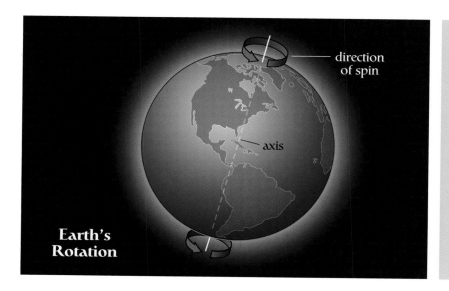

direction of spin

axis

Earth's Rotation

Earth rotates on its axis. The axis is not straight up and down. It's slightly tilted. That tilt is responsible for the seasons. In the Northern Hemisphere's summer, the North Pole is tilted toward the Sun and the South Pole is tilted away. Six months later, the Earth has moved halfway around the Sun, so the tilt and the seasons are reversed.

from the Sun. That means it gets less sunlight to warm it, even at perihelion.

The more the axis is tilted toward or away from the Sun, the more extreme our seasons are. The tilt also cycles. Over the course of forty-one thousand years, the tilt goes back and forth between about 21 and 24 degrees. Could this cycle combine with the changing shape of Earth's orbit and its varying distance from the Sun to produce the ice ages and warm periods? Climate models say yes.

HUMAN ACTIVITY AND CLIMATE CHANGE

Climate modeling is very important in the twenty-first century. It helps us understand how human activity can change weather patterns. One of the most important changes in modern times is the amount of carbon dioxide (CO_2) in Earth's atmosphere.

Our atmosphere is a mix of different kinds of gases. Some gases are more common than others. Scientists often measure the less common gases in parts per million, or ppm. In 2009 the atmosphere had 385 ppm of CO_2. Compared to other gases, the amount of CO_2 is tiny. The air we breathe contains 600 molecules of oxygen for each molecule of CO_2.

The air contains very little CO_2, but the gas is very important to the climate. It keeps our planet's warmth from escaping into space. Like the glass of a greenhouse, CO_2 allows sunlight to reach the ground below and holds in some of the heat from the Sun. Without CO_2's greenhouse effect, Earth's average temperature would be cooler by about 50°F (28°C).

CONTINENTAL Drift

Earth's climate depends on its terrain—the arrangement of the continents, oceans, lakes, mountains, glaciers, and ice caps. Land heats up and cools down faster than water. Ice, snow, and clouds reflect sunlight more than land and water. Areas with deserts, rain forests, and ice caps have different patterns of heating.

Earth's continents are always drifting, or moving. The motion is very slow but over millions of years, it adds up. To model the climate of when dinosaurs ruled Earth, scientists don't use a current world map. Instead, they arrange the continents as they were at that time.

We know that natural processes have changed the amount of CO_2 in the air over Earth's history. And those changes in CO_2 have caused changes in climate. During ice ages, the CO_2 level was lower and the planet was cooler. And during the tropical period when dinosaurs ruled Earth, the air had more CO_2. You might think a warmer planet might be a better one. But scientists are learning that adding more CO_2 to the air might be too much of a good thing—especially when we add it too fast.

Life on Earth is always changing. Plants and animals can adapt to different conditions by moving locations or by evolving. But evolution is a slow process. And sometimes the places where a creature can move are worse than where it is already.

That's why climate scientists are concerned about how fast humans have been adding CO_2 to the atmosphere by burning fossil fuels such as coal and oil. A hundred years ago, the CO_2 level was only 300 ppm. For the ten thousand years that human civilization existed before that, the amount of CO_2 in the air was between 280 and 300 ppm.

Fossil-fuel burning in the twentieth century raised the CO_2 level a remarkable 85 ppm. And if we keep burning fossil fuel at the same rate, CO_2 could rise to 650 ppm in your lifetime. Some climate models predict that if that happens, Earth's average temperature will rise more than 10°F (6°C) by the year 2100.

Ten degrees of global warming may not seem like much compared to the day-to-day changes you experience all the time. But if every day was 10°F warmer, think of how different the climate would be. Midwinter would be like late fall or early spring. And in most parts of the world, many days in midsummer would be dangerously hot.

Temperature changes are not our only concerns. Rainfall and snowfall patterns will also

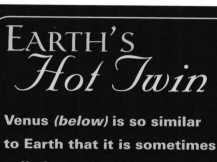

EARTH'S *Hot Twin*

Venus *(below)* is so similar to Earth that it is sometimes called our planet's twin. Without the greenhouse effect, its temperature would be suitable for human life. But its atmosphere is rich in CO_2 and traps so much heat that the planet's surface is hot enough to melt lead!

Computers were used to make this climate model of Earth's worldwide temperature in 2008. It is among the top ten warmest years since record keeping began in 1880. The model shows below-average temperatures in blue, average temperatures in white, and above-average temperatures in red.

change. Melting snow and ice feed many important rivers. So if there is less snow and ice to melt, many areas will have less water for drinking, washing, and irrigating farmland. Such changes in climate will force farmers around the world to change what they grow. Everywhere, the ecology—the mix of plants, animals, bacteria, and fungi—will change dramatically.

Climate models predict not only warmer weather but also more extreme conditions. And they also predict that the increase in average temperature will not be the same everywhere. The polar regions will probably have the greatest temperature rise. Large masses of ice will slowly melt and raise sea levels. That could be a major problem around the world because so many people live in cities and villages near seacoasts.

ARE CLIMATE MODELS CORRECT?

If the climate models are correct, humans are going to have to take steps to slow global warming. We'll have to make major changes in the way we live—and quickly.

This meeting of the Intergovernmental Panel on Climate Change took place in Bangkok, Thailand, in 2007.

To keep the CO_2 levels down, we'll have to stop burning so much fossil fuel. That will be difficult. We use those fuels for our homes, cars, factories, and most of our electricity.

But those predictions are only from models, and models might be incorrect. Should we really worry so much about what those models tell us? How do we know whether to make major changes or keep going as we have been?

To answer those questions, the United Nations Environment Programme and the World Meteorological Organization established the Intergovernmental Panel on Climate Change (IPCC) in 1988. The IPCC's main job is to keep us from acting on bad information. It doesn't rely on any single climate model. It looks at the predictions of the models from the world's best climate scientists using the world's most powerful computers.

The IPCC models all agree that the world is warming dramatically. They also agree that climate change can create very serious problems. But they disagree on how soon and in which ways we will have to act to prevent them.

World leaders would prefer more definite answers to make better decisions. But they realize that one set of questions often leads to another. Climate modelers have produced many important discoveries, but much more exploring lies ahead. The more they discover, the more likely we are to make decisions that are good for humanity—and for the world.

3

EXPLORING
the Moon

U.S. astronaut Buzz Aldrin
steps onto the surface of the
Moon in 1969. Aldrin was part
of the Apollo 11 space mission.

OVER THE CENTURIES, HUMANS SET FOOT ON EVERY CONTINENT AND SAILED EVERY SEA ON EARTH. AFTER ALL THAT, EXPLORING THE MOON BECAME THE ULTIMATE GOAL. BUT HOW COULD WE EVER TRAVEL TO THE MOON? IT SEEMED IMPOSSIBLE. BY THE MID-TWENTIETH CENTURY, HOWEVER, THINGS HAD BEGUN TO CHANGE. SCIENTISTS SENT THE FIRST ARTIFICIAL SATELLITES INTO ORBIT. AND THEY WORKED ON NEW TECHNOLOGY THAT WOULD ALLOW HUMANS TO TRAVEL BEYOND EARTH'S ATMOSPHERE.

U.S. scientist Eugene Shoemaker (1929–1997) realized that a trip to the Moon would soon be within human reach. And he set a personal goal to get there.

Eugene Shoemaker at work in Arizona in the mid-1960s

WHY GO TO THE MOON?

Shoemaker was a geologist—a scientist who studies Earth's history. Geologists often study rocks and land formations. In the 1950s, Shoemaker went to Arizona to investigate Barringer Crater. It was also known as Meteor Crater. A meteor is a space rock. But not everyone agreed that the Barringer Crater had formed when a space rock crashed to Earth. Shoemaker settled the question when he found certain minerals in the crater. Those minerals could only have formed under the sudden heat and pressure of an impact from space.

Craters fascinated him. He wanted to understand how they formed and what they could tell us about the 4.5-billion-year history of Earth.

At a mere fifty thousand years old, Meteor Crater was very young. Shoemaker wanted to study much older craters, but they were hard to find. Rain, wind, streams, and seasonal changes wore them away. And other geological changes destroyed them or made them nearly impossible to recognize.

That didn't stop Shoemaker. He knew that earlier in Earth's history, large numbers of rocks were bombarding our planet from space. At the same time,

The Barringer Crater in Arizona was probably created fifty thousand years ago by a meteorite. A meteorite is a space rock that strikes the surface of Earth.

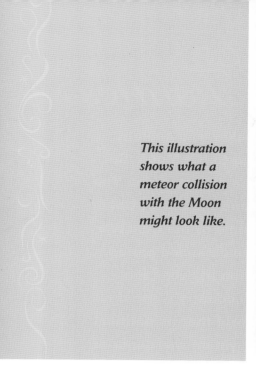

This illustration shows what a meteor collision with the Moon might look like.

they were also smashing into the Moon. So he decided to become the first geologist to study other worlds. He began to study the craters of the Moon from images taken through powerful telescopes.

Once those Moon craters formed, very little changed them. Space dust slowly wore down their sharp edges. But only another impact could change their shape. Shoemaker learned to read the craters of the Moon like you would read a history book.

The age of space exploration had not yet begun. But Shoemaker began planning the ultimate geological field trip. Late in his life, he described his plans.

> I had a personal ambition as a young man. I had the idea long before there was a space program that human beings would actually get to the Moon in the course of my lifetime. And I imagined that the principal reason in going to the Moon would be to study the geology. Why else would you go? So I had this game plan to try to be the first geologist to go to the Moon.

THE APOLLO PROGRAM

In 1961 John F. Kennedy was president of the United States. He set a goal for the National Aeronautics and Space Administration (NASA). Kennedy wanted

NASA to land a human astronaut on the Moon by the end of that decade. NASA named the mission Apollo after the Greek god of light.

Shoemaker developed a medical condition that kept him from becoming an astronaut. But that didn't end his ambition to explore the Moon's geology. He was eager to get involved in planning the Apollo missions.

Scientific discovery wasn't at the top of the president's list of reasons to go to the Moon. The United States would not have spent so much money on the Apollo program just to study geology. But something else was at stake—national pride. It was vital to be the first country to land astronauts on the Moon and return them safely. It would prove the country's technological leadership.

Shoemaker had a different view. Technological leadership was important. But so were scientific leadership and discovery. If Apollo astronauts set foot on the Moon, they would not return empty-handed.

THE MOON and Politics

Eugene Shoemaker saw geology as the reason to go to the Moon. But politicians had a different idea. The United States and the Soviet Union were in the middle of the Cold War (1945–1991)—an extended period of serious tension between the countries. Each country wanted to prove to the world that its political and economic system was superior. The race to land on the Moon was part of that competition.

Kennedy was determined that the United States would win the space race. On May 25, 1961, he declared, "I believe that this nation should commit itself to achieving the goal, before this decade is out, of landing a man on the Moon and returning him safely to the earth. No single space project in this period will be more impressive to mankind."

Shoemaker wanted to be sure the astronauts would collect the most useful lunar rock and soil samples. He wanted the astronauts to choose samples he himself would choose. So he jumped at the chance to teach geology to the Apollo astronauts.

On July 16, 1969, NASA launched the *Apollo 11* spacecraft from the Kennedy Space Center in Florida. Three astronauts were on board—Neil Armstrong, Edwin "Buzz" Aldrin, and Michael Collins.

> *"That's one small step for [a] man,*
> *one giant leap for mankind."*
> —Apollo 11 *astronaut Neil Armstrong, after setting foot on the Moon, July 20, 1969*

Three days after launch, *Apollo 11* was in orbit around the Moon. On July 20, 1969, Armstrong and Aldrin climbed into a smaller attached craft, the *Eagle*. They prepared to land it on the Moon. The *Eagle* approached its landing zone in the lunar region known as the Sea of Tranquility. On board the *Eagle* was a camera. It sent photos to TV screens back on Earth in NASA's mission control center. The black-and-white images showed close-ups of small craters as the *Eagle* swept past, its landing rockets kicking up clouds of moondust. Would the astronauts have enough fuel to land safely? Or would they have to return to the command module?

It was a close call, but they made it to the surface. Armstrong announced, "Tranquility Base here. The *Eagle* has landed." People around the world cheered. A few hours later, Armstrong—soon followed by Aldrin—stepped out onto the Moon. A few days after that, Armstrong, Aldrin, and Collins returned safely to Earth.

A GEOLOGIST'S DREAM

Kennedy's goal had been achieved, but Shoemaker's was just beginning. Armstrong and Aldrin had collected 48 pounds (22 kilograms) of rocks for geologists to analyze. Five other successful Apollo flights followed, each one to a different kind of lunar terrain. Each team of Apollo astronauts brought back more lunar rocks and soil than the team before.

Thanks to Shoemaker's teaching, the astronauts knew how to use basic geology tools. And they knew enough science to select interesting samples. Still, no one on the spaceflights was an expert geologist.

That changed in December 1972 with *Apollo 17*, the last spacecraft in the program to land on the Moon. That mission included geologist

This section of Moon rock was brought back to Earth by the Apollo 12 **astronauts.** Apollo 12 **landed on the Moon in 1970.**

Harrison Schmidt. He and astronaut Eugene Cernan collected more than 240 pounds (111 kg) of Moon rock and soil. That brought the Apollo collection to 2,415 samples weighing a total of 842 pounds (382 kg).

BACK TO THE MOON

After Apollo, lunar missions were less frequent. But scientists still wanted to learn about the Moon. Some scientists planned Moon bases where people could live for months or years. But those people would need water to survive, and they couldn't carry enough on their spacecraft to last for years. So scientists hoped to find sources of water on the Moon.

One of the first missions to look for water was NASA's Lunar Prospector. *Prospector* was developed in the 1990s to look for water at the Moon's south and north poles. Near the poles are craters whose bottoms are always in shadow, away from the heat of the Sun. They were perfect places to find ice that never melts.

Shoemaker was looking forward to the Prospector mission. In July 1997, he left for a trip to Australia to explore an asteroid (large space rock) impact site.

MOON ROCKS on Earth

The Soviet Union's unmanned Luna missions collected and returned a total of about 12 ounces (336 grams) of lunar rock and soil. Scientists compared the Apollo and Luna samples to more than 120 meteorites found on Earth. Those meteorites, weighing a total of more than 106 pounds (48 kg), were identified as pieces of the Moon.

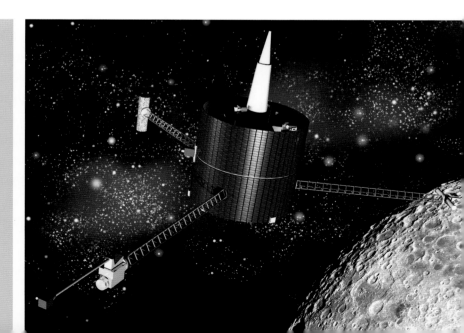

An artist created this image of Prospector *circling the Moon.* Prospector *was small. It had a diameter of 4 feet (1.3 m) and was 4.5 feet (1.4 m) tall. It had three masts that extended outward 8 feet (2.5 m). The masts carried scientific instruments.*

Unfortunately, he was killed in a car accident there. His body was cremated. In tribute, NASA made room for a small sample of his ashes to travel to the Moon with *Prospector*.

Prospector was launched on January 6, 1998. A week later, it settled into an orbit 62 miles (100 km) high. The orbit carried the spacecraft over the Moon's poles every 118 minutes.

Prospector's instruments showed hints of ice in those polar craters but no definite evidence. Its batteries began to die on July 31, 1999. NASA crash-landed the craft in the Shoemaker Crater near the lunar south pole. They hoped that the crash would send up a plume of water visible from Earth. The crash did not reveal any water. But Eugene Shoemaker had, in a way, achieved his personal dream of reaching the Moon.

The first decade of the twenty-first century was marked by a renewed interest in human missions to the Moon. In 2007 and 2008, Japan, China, and India sent scientific spacecraft there. In June 2009, the United States launched two satellites—an orbiter and an impactor—to continue *Prospector*'s work.

The United States also began planning Moon missions that will serve as practice for sending humans to Mars by around 2040. The plans included building a lunar space port, where rockets carrying humans would be launched toward Mars.

Perhaps Eugene Cernan will live long enough to see humans set foot on the Moon again. That will fulfill the hopes of his final words on lunar soil: "We leave the Moon at Taurus-Littrow [a lunar valley] . . . as we came and, God willing, as we shall return, with peace and hope for all mankind. Godspeed the crew of *Apollo 17*."

4 INTERPLANETARY Exploration

New Horizons *spacecraft blasts off aboard the*
Atlas V *rocket from the John F. Kennedy Space*
Center in Florida in 2006. The craft is on its way
to explore the outer limits of the solar system.

$\mathcal{T}$HE APOLLO PROGRAM WILL ALWAYS RANK AS
ONE OF THE MOST DARING EXPLORATIONS IN HISTORY. BUT IT IS STILL THE
SMALLEST STEP WE WILL EVER TAKE IN TRAVELING TO OTHER WORLDS.

We humans have already explored far beyond the Moon—not in person but by machine. Our spacecraft have landed on or flown near asteroids, comets, all seven other major planets, and numerous moons. We have already begun missions to explore the farthest reaches of the solar system.

VISITING OTHER WORLDS

The first interplanetary (between planets) missions aimed for Venus and Mars. They are Earth's nearest neighbors. Venus is similar to Earth in size and makeup. The more we know about Venus, the better we can understand Earth. For example, Venus's size and distance from the Sun would make it suitable for Earthlike life—except for one thing. It has a "runaway" greenhouse effect from the large concentration of carbon dioxide in its atmosphere.

On February 12, 1961, the Soviet Union launched *Venera 1 (below)*, an unmanned space probe. The probe lost radio contact after a week.

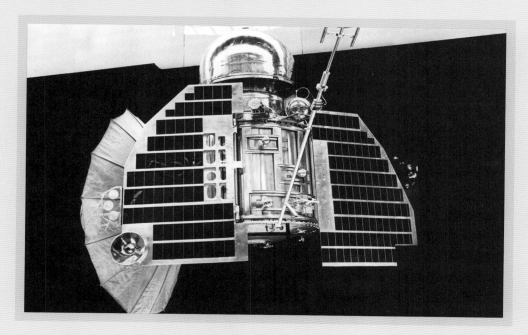

But it was on a path that took it within 60,000 miles (100,000 km) of Venus. That's about one-quarter as far as the Moon is from Earth.

Not long after, the United States launched a probe, *Mariner 1*. It went badly off course and had to be destroyed less than five minutes after liftoff on July 22, 1962. But its backup, *Mariner 2*, launched successfully on August 27, 1962. It sent back measurements from within 21,000 miles (34,000 km) of Venus on December 14 of that year.

Mariner 2's instruments showed that Venus's cloud tops were cool. But the surface of the planet was at least 800°F (425°C). That ruled out any hope of finding life or landing humans there. More recent measurements place the temperature even higher—865°F (462°C).

Missions to Mars soon followed. Again, the first U.S. and Soviet attempts failed. The first Martian success was a 1964 flyby made by the U.S. *Mariner 4*. Its close-up pictures of Mars showed a dry and cratered surface. If any organisms lived there, they were probably simple life-forms hidden underground.

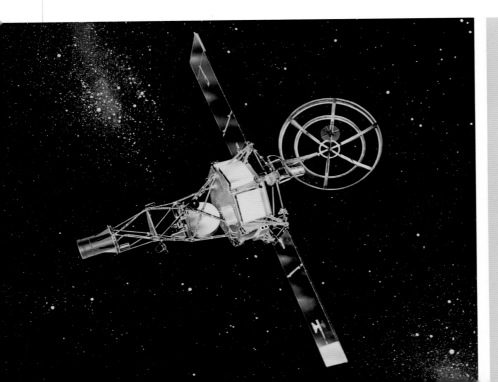

This is an illustration of Mariner 2. In 1962 it passed within about 21,000 miles (34,000 km) of Venus.

New Horizons

In January 2006, the New Horizons mission blasted off toward a distant region of the solar system known as the Kuiper Belt. It will reach its first target, the dwarf planet Pluto, in 2015. It will study that icy world and its moons, Charon, Nix, and Hydra. Then it will continue on to study other Kuiper Belt objects (KBOs).

Pluto was still considered a planet when the *New Horizons* probe left Earth. Seven months later, the International Astronomical Union (IAU) demoted it to dwarf planet status. But that didn't change the importance of the mission. Whether we call Pluto a planet, a dwarf planet, or a KBO, it remains a fascinating target to explore.

Meanwhile, other missions to Mars have been making different discoveries. The *Mars Global Surveyor* sent data to Earth from its Mars orbit between 1996 through 2006. It produced detailed maps of Mars's terrain and minerals. The 2008 *Phoenix* lander found and made measurements of ice just beneath the surface in Mars's Arctic region.

Space agencies around the world are planning future missions to Mars. According to long-range plans, those missions will include human astronauts sometime around the year 2040.

The Phoenix *lander's Surface Stereo Imager took this photo of the lander's solar panel* (left) *and robotic arm* (right). *The arm is scooping up a sample of Martian soil.*

5 THE *Hubble Space Telescope*

The Hubble Space Telescope orbits above Earth. Information gathered by the telescope has expanded our understanding of the solar system and beyond.

$\mathcal{L}$ONG BEFORE HUMANS SENT SPACECRAFTS

INTO THE SOLAR SYSTEM, WE STUDIED THE PLANETS WITH TELESCOPES.

IN FACT, ASTRONOMERS WITH TELESCOPES DISCOVERED THE PLANETS

URANUS AND NEPTUNE, ASTEROIDS, AND KBOS SUCH AS PLUTO.

Telescopes also gave us a new window on the universe beyond the solar system. For example, we realized that the Sun is a slightly larger-than-average star. The better our telescopes became, the more stars we could see and the more we could learn about them.

We attached other instruments called spectroscopes to our telescopes. Each star's light contains a mix of colors. That mix is called a spectrum (*pl.* spectra). Spectroscopes analyzed the stars' spectra. Those spectra told us what stars were made of and how they produced their light and heat.

No telescope in history has changed astronomy faster and more completely than the Hubble Space Telescope. This wonder of exploration technology has changed the way we look at the universe.

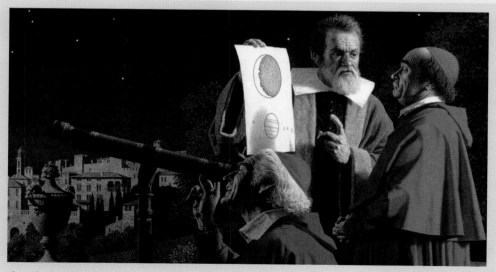

A painting shows Italian astronomer Galileo Galilei (1564–1642) explaining his discoveries about the Moon. He was among the first to explore the night sky with a telescope.

Edwin Hubble's Universe

While most other astronomers were studying stars and planets, Edwin Hubble (1889–1953) focused his telescopes on blurry objects called nebulas. In the 1920s, he recognized that most of the nebulas are very distant, very large systems of stars. He also realized that our Sun and stars are part of the same kind of system—we are just seeing the system close-up.

Astronomers named such a collection of stars a galaxy. And they named our own galaxy after the band of stars we see at its faraway edge—the Milky Way.

Hubble's most important discovery came from examining the spectra of galaxies. He found that the color of a galaxy changes as the galaxy moves. Think of an ambulance or police siren. When the siren is moving toward you, it has one pitch (higher or lower sound). The pitch changes as the siren moves past and away from you. In the same way, the spectrum of the stars in a moving galaxy changes colors. If a galaxy is moving toward Earth, the spectrum is bluer. If it is moving away, it shifts toward red.

By 1929 Hubble discovered that only a few of the very closest galaxies showed a blueshift. All the rest were redshifted. Most important, he found that the farther away a galaxy was, the more its light was redshifted. He even developed a formula called Hubble's Law. If you know the distance of a galaxy from Earth, Hubble's Law tells you what its redshift is.

Edwin Hubble gazes through a telescope at the Mount Wilson Observatory in California in 1937.

Spilled Milk

The word *galaxy* comes from the Greek word *galaxias*, meaning "milky." Our own galaxy is named for the Milky Way, because its distant edge looks like milk spilled across the sky.

Red Shift, Blue Shift

Edwin Hubble's study of galaxies showed that a few of the nearest galaxies have blueshifted light. That means they are moving toward us. But if the universe is expanding, why don't all galaxies move away from one another? The answer is that galaxies form clusters held together by gravity. Galaxies in the same cluster may be moving toward or away from one another. Thus the light from galaxies near us—our Local Group—can appear redshifted or blueshifted. But two clusters are always moving apart. Thus the light we see from galaxies outside of the Local Group is redshifted.

And that works the other way around too. If you know a galaxy's redshift, you can determine its distance from Earth.

Hubble's findings had a simple but surprising explanation—the universe is expanding. He couldn't say what is causing the expansion. But it is a fact. That discovery has made Hubble one of the most famous astronomers of all time. His work was so important that NASA named one of its most historic missions, the Hubble Space Telescope (HST), in his honor.

Why Put a Telescope in Space?

Most people love to see the twinkling of the stars on a clear night. But astronomers know that stars don't really twinkle. Like the Sun, stars put out a steady stream of light. However, for that light to reach our eyes—or our telescopes—it has to pass through Earth's atmosphere.

The air in our atmosphere bends the starlight's path just a little bit. The amount of bending changes with the temperature and pressure of the air. The starlight changes as the conditions of the air change. That's the twinkling we see, and it makes telescope images less sharp than they could be.

The atmosphere also interferes with our observations in other ways. The atmosphere is filled with energy called electromagnetic waves. Light is one type of electromagnetic wave. But there are many forms of electromagnetic waves. And the visible spectrum—the range of colors we can see—is part of a broader electromagnetic spectrum.

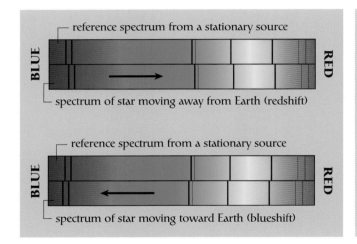

reference spectrum from a stationary source

BLUE ... RED

spectrum of star moving away from Earth (redshift)

reference spectrum from a stationary source

BLUE ... RED

spectrum of star moving toward Earth (blueshift)

This diagram shows what Hubble measured when it passed light from galaxies through its spectroscope. The pattern of dark lines is produced when the coolest gases on the outside of a star absorb some of the light from the inside. Each type of atom produces its own recognizable pattern. If the source of light is moving rapidly away from or toward Earth, that pattern shifts toward the red or blue end of the spectrum.

Electromagnetic waves are a back-and-forth pulsing of electricity and magnetism that travels through space. Those waves have many different wavelengths. A wavelength is the space between one pulse and the next.

The wavelength of visible light is very short. Red light has the longest wavelength of all visible colors. Still, about 33,000 deep red wavelengths could fit in an inch (about 13,000 in a centimeter). The wavelength of blue/violet light is about half as long (about 65,000 waves to the inch, or about 25,000 to the centimeter).

Beyond the visible part of the spectrum are other forms of electromagnetic waves. On the long wavelength end, just beyond red, is infrared light. Then come microwaves and radio waves.

On the short wavelength end, past blue and violet, is ultraviolet light. The wavelengths of X-rays and gamma rays are even shorter. Earth's atmosphere allows visible light to pass through, but it blocks some longer and shorter electromagnetic waves.

Putting a telescope in orbit above the atmosphere avoids that blockage. The telescope's position above the atmosphere also eliminates twinkling, so the visible light images it captures are sharper. And a telescope in orbit can detect infrared or ultraviolet light that never reaches Earth's surface.

Space telescopes are really orbiting observatories. They do much more than collect and focus light. They also have devices to analyze the light, such as ultraviolet and infrared spectroscopes. The spectra tell them how much of certain chemical elements are present in stars or what gases make up the atmospheres of planets. Infrared spectra can also be used to measure the temperature patterns on planets and moons.

Many early satellites carried small telescopes. Those were better than earthbound instruments for certain observations. But in most cases, they were too small to collect much light. Large ground-based telescopes were still much better for most jobs.

Scientists knew that the ideal telescope would be a combination—a large telescope that traveled in space. In the 1970s, NASA astronomers and engineers began designing the HST. It would be a full-scale space observatory. An observatory always needs maintenance. At that time, NASA had just begun building space shuttles to carry people and heavy loads into space. So NASA designed the HST to be launched and serviced by space shuttle astronauts.

HUBBLE TROUBLES AND TRIUMPHS

The story of the HST is full of struggle and success. At first, NASA hoped to launch it in 1983. But designing and building it took longer than expected. Then it was targeted for an October 1986 launch when tragedy struck.

On January 28 of that year, space shuttle *Challenger* was launched from the Kennedy Space Center in Florida. Less than two minutes after launch, the shuttle exploded. Its crew of seven all died. NASA managers canceled all space shuttle flights until they could understand and fix the problem that had caused the explosion. The long-awaited launch of the HST was put on hold.

The HST was finally launched in spring 1990 and reached orbit on April 24. Within a few weeks, astronomers knew the HST had a major problem. The

Smoke trails filled the sky after the space shuttle Challenger *exploded on January 28, 1986.*

Hubble's mirror had been made precisely—but it was the wrong shape! That made the Hubble images blurry.

Fixing the problem required special equipment and work by astronauts to install it. But it was worth it. In December 1993, the HST began sending spectacular images back to Earth. Astronomers still continue to make revolutionary discoveries from its data.

Every mission has to come to an end, and the HST is no exception. After its final servicing mission in 2009, the HST is expected to operate for about five more years. But eventually, a gyroscope (a device to keep the telescope pointing in a particular direction) or a main computer will fail, and astronomers won't be able to use the HST anymore.

OTHER SPACE TELESCOPES

The HST is the first and most famous of NASA's four orbiting "great observatories." The Compton Gamma Ray Observatory (CGRO), the Chandra X-ray Telescope, and the Spitzer Space Telescope are the other three. Each one observes the universe in different parts of the electromagnetic spectrum. Each part of the spectrum gives astronomers different information about the objects they are observing.

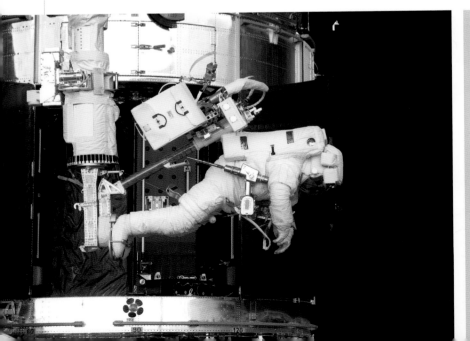

During a space walk to service the Hubble, an astronaut floats into position.

Light from the Andromeda galaxy, the Milky Way's nearest neighbor, is slightly blueshifted, though it takes a spectroscope to notice.

The HST does most of its work in visible light (the colors we can see), infrared light, and ultraviolet light. The CGRO was launched in 1991. It had four instruments that covered a wide range of the electromagnetic spectrum. The CGRO's mission ended in 2000. The Gamma Ray Large Area Space Telescope (GLAST) replaced it in 2008.

The Chandra X-ray Telescope was launched in 1999. As its name suggests, it observes in the X-ray part of the spectrum. The Spitzer Space Telescope is an infrared observatory. It was launched in 2003. It used liquid helium to detect long infrared wavelengths from cold, distant objects. In 2009 it ran out of the liquid helium. But it continues to observe warmer but still very chilly (or extremely redshifted) bodies in the solar system and beyond.

NASA and other space agencies have plans for several other major space telescopes. NASA's James Webb Space Telescope (JWST) will be launched in about 2013. Like the Spitzer, the JWST will observe in the infrared. So it is not an exact replacement for the HST. Fortunately, many of the newest ground-based telescopes can adjust to correct for twinkling. That means Hubble's work in visible light can be replaced. But no major instruments are planned to replace its ultraviolet observations.

Space telescopes have given us great knowledge of the objects in the cosmos (the universe). But Edwin Hubble's discovery of the expanding universe has also led to a different kind of exploration—to the most distant parts of the cosmos and back to the very beginning of time.

MAPPING THE
Cosmos

The light from the most distant regions of the universe reaches Earth as microwaves. To study this light, scientists launched two space observatories—the Cosmic Background Explorer (COBE) and the Wilkinson Microwave Anisotropy Probe (WMAP, above).

Some supernovas involve stars called white dwarfs. Before exploding, a white dwarf (above right) draws material from a companion star. Scientists know the point at which a white dwarf will explode, and they know how much energy the explosion produces. By measuring the brightness of the explosion, they can calculate how far it is from Earth.

They also computed how fast the galaxy was moving away by measuring its redshift. For every galaxy, the speed was faster than Hubble's Law predicted. The expansion of the universe seemed to be speeding up! What does that result mean? One explanation is that the universe is filled with "dark energy" that works against gravity. Gravity slows down the expansion of galaxies, but dark energy speeds it up. Scientists have a few ideas about what exactly dark energy is, but they are far from certain.

From the Cosmic to the Subatomic

To test their ideas about dark energy, cosmologists need to know more about what happened during the big bang. If only they could study the way matter behaved under those extreme conditions, they might begin to find an answer.

It turns out that they can! But instead of thinking big, they need to think both big and small. They need to use some of the world's most colossal machines to probe the world of subatomic particles. These particles are smaller than atoms (the particles that make up ordinary matter).

7 THE *Large Hadron Collider*

A section of the Large Hadron Collider (LHC) is lowered into a specially constructed pit. The collider is one of the largest machines ever built.

$\mathcal{T}$O MAKE SENSE OF THE BIG BANG, COSMOLOGISTS NEEDED TO KNOW HOW MATTER BEHAVES WHEN THERE IS SO MUCH OF IT IN SO LITTLE SPACE. TO UNDERSTAND WHAT THEY WERE FACING, WE NEED TO START WITH ONE OF SCIENCE'S OLDEST QUESTIONS. WHAT IS MATTER? TO FOLLOW THAT QUESTION, WE WILL LEAVE THE REALM OF THE VERY LARGE (COSMOLOGY) AND ENTER THE REALM OF THE VERY SMALLEST PARTICLES KNOWN. TO EXPLORE THIS WORLD, WE WILL NEED ONE OF THE LARGEST, MOST POWERFUL, AND MOST COMPLEX MACHINES EVER BUILT—THE LARGE HADRON COLLIDER (LHC).

THE MATTER OF MATTER

To understand the LHC and what it does, we need to start with what we know about matter. Ordinary matter is made of atoms, and atoms join together to make molecules. Iron is made of iron atoms. The oxygen we breathe is made of pairs of oxygen atoms joined together into an oxygen molecule. The water we drink is made of molecules each containing two hydrogen atoms and one oxygen atom.

The force holding atoms and molecules together is electricity. Atoms carry electric charges. Electric charges come in two types that we call positive and negative. Opposite charges attract each other. Two charges of the same type push each other apart.

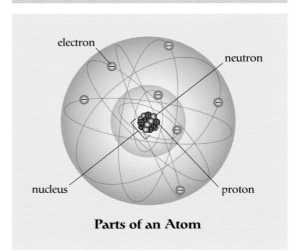

This illustration shows the electrically charged parts of an atom (electrons and protons), as well as the neutral particles called neutrons.

Parts of an Atom

But there is more to matter than atoms. Physicists (scientists who study matter and energy) have discovered that atoms are made of smaller particles. And they have discovered other particles of matter that are not parts of atoms.

Most of an atom's mass is concentrated in a tiny positively charged center called a nucleus (*pl.* nuclei). Surrounding that nucleus are very lightweight, negatively charged particles called electrons.

Inside nuclei are two types of smaller particles. Those particles are called protons and neutrons. (Protons are positively charged, and neutrons are electrically neutral.) To build all the atoms in the universe, it seems you need only these three types of particles—electrons, protons, and neutrons. Because they are smaller than atoms, the particles are called subatomic.

The most important difference between one kind of atom and another is the number of protons in its nucleus. Every hydrogen atom has one proton. Every carbon atom has six protons. Every oxygen atom has eight protons. And every uranium atom has ninety-two protons.

Electrons and nuclei are all that chemists need to explain the way atoms and molecules react with each other. In a chemical reaction, atoms rearrange themselves to form different molecules. But the atoms and their nuclei do not change.

More than Chemistry

Matter, however, can change in ways other than simple chemical reactions. Sometimes, atoms do change into other kinds of atoms. The change begins inside the atom when the nucleus sends out (or emits) a piece of itself. That process is called radioactivity, or radiation.

In the 1930s, physicists studying radioactivity discovered another type of subatomic particle. They called it a neutrino. A neutrino is so tiny that it has almost no mass at all. It isn't part of an atom, but it can be created inside a nucleus. The proton, neutron, electron, and neutrino make up atomic matter. But the universe has many other kinds of subatomic particles that are not part of atoms. Those particles were first discovered by scientists who studied cosmic rays. Cosmic rays are very fast-moving particles that strike Earth from space. The physicists who first studied them found some very unusual particles.

Physicists realized that cosmic rays were opening a new window of knowledge about matter. Since the particles came from space, they might also teach us something about how the universe worked. Physicists wanted

This illustration shows how cosmic rays strike Earth's atmosphere and produce a variety of subatomic particles.

to learn more about cosmic ray particles. But the particles arrive from space unpredictably. So the physicists looked for ways to make their own.

MADE-TO-ORDER COSMIC RAYS

Scientists created machines called particle accelerators that imitate the way nature makes cosmic rays. What exactly are the machines imitating, and how do they do it?

Outer space is quite empty compared to Earth's atmosphere. But many of the particles in space are moving very fast. A steady stream of high-energy protons, helium nuclei, and electrons bombards Earth from space. Many of these come from the Sun. But others come from other stars and even other galaxies. Some are moving very close to the speed of light. Those are called primary cosmic rays.

When those primary cosmic rays collide with the atoms of Earth's atmosphere, they create other particles. Those are called secondary cosmic rays. Secondary cosmic rays include many kinds of subatomic particles that do not exist in atoms. Physicists can use accelerators to create and study those kinds of particles. In doing so, they hope to learn more about matter and energy of all kinds.

A particle accelerator does its work in several steps. First, it creates a beam of artificial primary cosmic rays. Then it creates a collision between that beam and a target. The result is artificial secondary cosmic rays with many of the unusual subatomic particles of interest. Physicists then detect and measure those unusual particles.

FROM CYCLOTRONS TO COLLIDERS

So how does an accelerator create a beam of cosmic rays? It takes atoms and uses electricity to strip away their electrons. Then it injects either the negatively charged electrons or the remaining positively charged nuclei into an airless tube. In the tube, a very strong electric field or voltage (similar to a battery but much more powerful) speeds up the electrons or nuclei.

One trip through the electric field is not nearly enough. All accelerators work by adding a little energy step-by-step. Some devices, called linear

accelerators, have a long lineup of acceleration sections. But many other accelerators send particles on a circular path. The first major accelerator used the circular approach. It began its work in the late 1930s. It was called the cyclotron. And for decades, all the great accelerators in the world used a similar design.

The cyclotron has a large airless circular chamber placed between the poles of a powerful electromagnet. An electromagnet is a coil of wire that carries a strong electric current. That coil produces a magnetic field just as a bar magnet does.

The magnet forces the charged particles to travel in a circular path. The chamber is split into two semicircles called dees (after the letter *D*). An electric generator creates a large alternating voltage across the gap between the dees. *Alternating* means that the voltage switches back and forth from positive to negative. As the particles arrive at one side of the gap, the voltage gives them an energy boost.

By the time the particles complete a half circle and reach the other side of the gap, the voltage has reversed to give them another boost. As they gain energy, they go in larger and larger circles. When the circle grows as large as the chamber, the beam is sent out to strike a target.

The beam works like primary cosmic rays. Since the scientists know when and where the collision occurs, they can put a detector in the right place. Things happen very fast, so the detector needs to operate at just the right time. It also needs to preserve a record of the path of the particles created in the collision.

Over the history of particle accelerators, many different kinds of detectors have been developed. The best modern detectors produce sparks along the path of a particle. Each type of particle can be recognized by the shape of its path and the way it sometimes transforms or splits into other particles. Physicists can also determine how fast and in what direction the particle was going.

One of the goals of accelerators is to discover particles that have never been seen before. That means putting more energy into each collision. One way to do that is to make the circular path longer. Another is to use stronger electromagnets to make the path tighter. Another is to use heavier nuclei. And still another is to create a collider where two beams meet head-on. All of those techniques have come together in the world's newest and most powerful particle accelerator—the LHC.

LETTER BY LETTER

When most people learn what *LHC* stands for, they don't have much trouble with the first and last letters. They know what *large* means, and they know about collisions. But they might not know what a hadron is. They also don't know whether *large* refers to the machine or hadrons. So let's take a closer look at the LHC to answer those questions letter by letter.

The red circle outlines the area under which the LHC runs.

WHAT IS *a Hadron*

In the 1960s, physicists such as Murray Gell-Mann began to see a pattern in the properties of subatomic particles. Gell-Mann explained the pattern with a new theory. The theory stated that protons, neutrons, and many other subatomic particles are made up of even smaller particles called quarks. The exceptions were lightweight particles, such as electrons and neutrinos. Physicists began using the word *hadron* (from the Greek *adros*, meaning "bulky") to describe particles composed of quarks. The LHC will accelerate hadrons as small as protons and as large as lead nuclei.

The *C*, for "collider," tells us that the machine accelerates two beams of subatomic particles in opposite directions. Subatomic particles are classified in several ways. Hadrons are one classification. That's the *H* in LHC. After the hadrons have reached nearly the speed of light, the beams collide head-on.

The L, for "large," refers to the size of the machine. To build such great speed, the beams are accelerated around a loop. The LHC lies inside a concrete tunnel about 12 feet (3.8 m) in diameter. The tunnel is 160 to 570 feet (50 to 175 m) underground. It is made up of eight smaller curved segments called arcs. The arcs are joined together by straight segments called insertions. One trip around the tunnel is 17 miles (27 km).

The tunnel was originally built between 1983 and 1988 for a different accelerator called the Large Electron-Positron Collider. Physicists and engineers are always planning bigger and more powerful accelerators. Because their projects are so expensive, they can't always find the money to start or complete the job. So when the Large Electron-Positron Collider had completed its work, scientists looked for other ways to use the valuable tunnel.

During the 1980s and early 1990s, it looked as if the United States was going to build a giant collider. It would be called the Superconducting Super Collider (SSC). Physicists around the world were very disappointed when the U.S. Congress canceled the partially completed project in 1993 because of its cost.

But the physicists didn't give up. In 1995 the European Organization for Nuclear Research in Switzerland (called CERN for its French name) approved the design of the LHC. Its completion was planned for 2005.

The cost of building the LHC was shared by sixty countries whose scientists will use it. The tunnel crosses the border between Switzerland and France four times, so it's a good thing that hadrons don't need passports! Like many large engineering projects, it took longer than expected to complete. LHC scientists produced their first test beams on September 10, 2008.

A major failure nine days later shut down the machine for more than a year of repairs. But physicists such as Monica Dunford of the University of Chicago's Enrico Fermi Institute are confident that the problems can be taken care of and that the LHC will succeed. Its explorations may transform the science of the subatomic universe just as the repaired Hubble Space Telescope's discoveries transformed astronomy.

SUPEREXPENSIVE *Super Collider*

In 1991 the United States began tunneling underground near Waxahachie, Texas. A giant particle accelerator called the Superconducting Super Collider (SSC) was being constructed. Physicists started planning the project years before, in 1983. Congress approved it in 1987. The plan called for 54 miles (87 km) of tunnels. Unfortunately, by 1993, the estimated cost of the SSC had tripled. With nearly a quarter of the tunnel completed, Congress canceled the project.

LHC SCIENCE AND TECHNOLOGY

The LHC is one of the most complex machines ever built. To produce some of the world's most advanced scientific results, it needs many of the world's most advanced technologies. To Dunford, that makes the LHC both very big and very small. Her research projects use a detector called ATLAS. ATLAS is five stories high. But it is built from millions of very small, precisely made, sensitive parts.

"Imagine a very expensive handmade watch," she explains. "That watch is made up of very small gears and parts that must fit together precisely for the watch to work. A good watchmaker could make such a watch in several days. Now imagine if that watch was five stories tall but was still full of the same very small gears and parts. How many days would it take the watchmaker to make such a watch? To build ATLAS, it took several thousand people over ten years."

One of the most advanced technologies in the LHC is its magnets. Electromagnets guide and control the LHC's particle beams.

The LHC's electromagnets are among the most powerful in the world. They come in two types that serve two different purposes. To keep the beam on track, each arc of the LHC contains 154 enormous and powerful steering magnets (1,232 in all). Those magnets guide the beam around the arcs' curves.

The particles in the beam all have the same electric charge, so they repel one another. Thus the LHC tunnel has 392 more magnets that produce a squeezing force to keep the beam from spreading out. The squeezing magnets have four magnetic poles instead of two. They are between one-third and one-half the size of the steering magnets. Both types of magnet have equally intense magnetic fields.

LHC was built to answer the most important questions about the nature of matter. The collision of two high-energy particles often creates new particles.

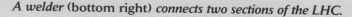

A welder (bottom right) *connects two sections of the LHC.*

The LHC scientists make sure collisions happen at one of four special places around the LHC loop where special detectors produce images of the particles' paths. They often see events that take place in unimaginably short times. Some subatomic particles split or transform into other particles within a trillionth of a second or less.

Some particles occur so rarely or last for such short times that scientists need to examine millions of images to understand them. Fortunately, they have computer programs that can analyze images and call attention to the most interesting ones.

RE-CREATING THE BIG BANG

The collision of two high-energy hadron beams in the LHC will occur in a very small region. Within that region will be the highest concentration of matter and energy that scientists have ever seen. In fact, such conditions have not existed anywhere in the cosmos since the big bang.

For Dunford, that is one of the most exciting explorations made possible by the LHC. It will give cosmologists real data to test their theories of how the universe began and developed. It will almost surely raise important new

LHC Magnets

Each LHC magnet is enormous. The steering magnets are about 50 feet (15 m) long and weigh about 40 tons (35 metric tons). Inside each magnet are wires that carry an electrical current. The current creates its powerful magnetic field. Each magnet uses more electrical current than what is needed to power 13,000 100-watt lightbulbs. That much current would make an ordinary copper wire (such as the kind used in houses and offices) so hot that it would melt. The LHC magnets use a special electrical cable called superconducting wire. The superconducting wires work at extremely low temperatures, so the magnets can be kept cool with liquid helium.

"The adventure of building the LHC will end and a new adventure of discovery will begin."
—LHC project leader Lyndon Evans, at the LHC inauguration ceremony, October 21, 2008

questions. And those questions will probably lead to new and different observations with instruments such as WMAP.

SEARCHING FOR THE HIGGS

During the twentieth century, physicists discovered more and more types of particles. This growing list became known as the particle zoo. Physicists measured many different properties of the particles. And they looked for ways to use those properties to organize the particles into groups.

One of those properties was mass. Many of the unusual particles resembled familiar ones but had a different mass. For example, subatomic particles called the muon, the sigma, and the lambda were discovered in cosmic rays between 1937 and 1953. They seemed to be oversized versions of the electron, the proton, and the neutron. Scientists wondered what makes those newly discovered particles heavier. In fact, they wondered what gives *any* particle its mass.

British physicist Peter Higgs tried to answer that question. In 1964 Higgs came up with a theory. That theory predicted that there was a new kind of particle that scientists hadn't found yet. The particle was named the Higgs boson. The theory made sense, and physicists have been trying to find the Higgs boson ever since.

Dunford is one of those Higgs hunters. She thinks the LHC may find it. But she knows exploring is full of surprises. If the LHC does not discover the Higgs, she and thousands of other LHC physicists from all over the world will have to look for other explanations of why we have mass.

They will probably start by figuring out where Higgs's ideas are right and where they need to be changed. They will start by reexamining a system for organizing the particle zoo called the Standard Model. The Standard Model places particles in three

Peter Higgs visits the LHC in April 2008. Some experiments planned for the LHC will test his theories about the Higgs boson.

groups called generations. The first generation is normal matter. The particles of the second generation are heavier than the first. And the third generation is still heavier.

Scientists have some very good reasons to believe the Standard Model is on the right track. As the Standard Model developed, it predicted that certain particles existed, even though they had not been found yet. Scientists needed new research technologies, such as accelerators with higher energies or better detectors, to detect those particles.

With each improvement in accelerator technology, they found some predicted particles. They also found some surprises. Each unexpected discovery helped them improve the theory. And each discovery made Higgs's idea more important.

But one major problem remained. No one had ever actually found the Higgs boson, even using large accelerators. That's where the LHC comes in. Scientists believe that if the Higgs boson exists, the LHC will produce enough energy to find it.

The LHC marks a crossroads for subatomic physics. If the giant accelerator finds the Higgs boson, scientists will be eager to learn more about it. But if the Higgs boson does not appear, scientists will have to take a careful look at the Standard Model.

Either way, subatomic physics will begin a new quest. And subatomic physicists will eagerly develop new technologies to continue their exploration deep into the heart of matter.

THE QUARK AND *Lepton Ladder*

The Standard Model of particle physics groups particles into generations. Each generation has two quarks and two light particles called leptons. The first generation is normal matter. Its quarks are called up and down, and its leptons are the electron and the neutrino. The second generation is heavier than the first. It has quarks called strange and charm. Its leptons are the muon and the muon-neutrino. The third generation is the heaviest of all. Its quarks are called top and bottom, and its leptons are the tau and tau-neutrino. A 2002 discovery in a Canadian underground neutrino detector showed that three generations are enough to complete the Standard Model.

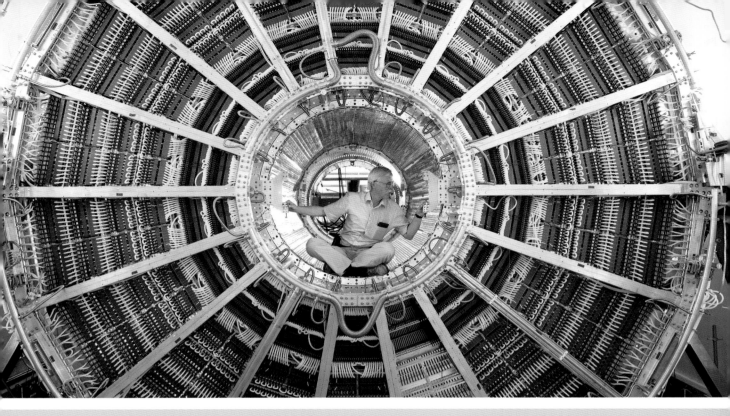

This structure (above) is a detector for the LHC. The illustration (below) *depicts what happens when two very energetic protons collide. The collision produces many different kinds of particles represented by the different colors. Scientists use advanced detectors and computers to analyze the paths of those particles. It takes many millions of collision events to determine the mass and other properties of newly discovered particles.*

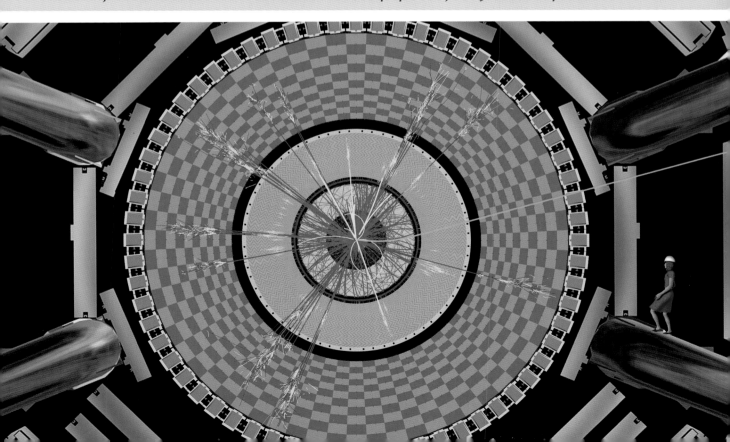

TIMELINE

1910	Cosmic rays are discovered.
1929	Edwin Hubble publishes a scientific paper describing the expanding universe.
1931	Georges Lemaître theorizes that all the matter in the universe was once squeezed together in a single point.
1949	Astronomer Fred Hoyle coins the term *big bang*.
1961	U.S. president John F. Kennedy vows to send astronauts to the Moon by the end of the decade.
1964	*Alvin* begins operation. Peter Higgs proposes the existence of the Higgs's boson.
1965	Arno Penzias and Robert Wilson detect cosmic background radiation.
1969	U.S. astronauts aboard *Apollo 11* land on the Moon.
1970s	Scientists begin designing the Hubble Space Telescope.
1976	Two U.S. Viking spacecraft land on Mars.
1977	*Alvin* discovers undersea vents near the Galápagos Islands. The United States launches two Voyager spacecraft toward the outer planets.
1986	*Alvin* explores the wreckage of RMS *Titanic* in the North Atlantic Ocean.
1988	The United Nations and the World Meteorological Organization establish the Intergovernmental Panel on Climate Change.
1989	NASA launches the Cosmic Background Explorer (COBE) satellite.
1990	The Hubble Space Telescope (HST) is launched.
1997	NASA's *Pathfinder* spacecraft lands on Mars.
1998	NASA launches the *Lunar Prospector* to look for ice on the Moon. Cosmologists discover that the expansion of the universe is speeding up.
2001	The Wilkinson Microwave Anisotropy Probe begins orbiting Earth.
2004	NASA lands rovers *Spirit* and *Opportunity* on Mars.
2006	The New Horizons mission is launched to explore the Kuiper belt.
2007	Japan, China, and India begin to send spacecraft into lunar orbit.
2008	The Large Hadron Collider (LHC) begins operating in Switzerland. It soon shuts down because of a magnet failure.
2009	Technical problems delay the restart of the LHC. Scientists record 385 ppm of carbon dioxide in Earth's atmosphere. The final Hubble Space Telescope repair mission is completed.

CHOOSE AN EIGHTH WONDER

Now that you've read about these seven wonders of exploration technology, do a little research to choose an eighth wonder. You may enjoy working with a friend.

To do your research, use the websites and books listed on pages 76 and 77. Think about other places on Earth, in the solar system, in the Milky Way galaxy, or in the universe that are within reach of human exploration. Research the instruments or technologies we can or will use to investigate them.

If you find the right questions, they may inspire you to gather photos and write your own chapter about an eighth wonder of exploration technology!

GLOSSARY

atmosphere: the gases surrounding a planet or moon

atom: the smallest particle of matter that can be a chemical element

big bang: the event that began the universe or the theory describing that event

climate model: a computer program for studying how Earth's climate might change

cosmic microwave background (CMB): the distant glow of the big bang that astronomers can detect in every direction from Earth

cosmic rays: fast-moving particles that strike the atoms of Earth's upper atmosphere and the particles that result from those collisions

cosmology: the study of how the universe formed and developed

dark energy: a phenomenon that seems to speed up the expansion of the universe

deep submergence vehicle (DSV): a vessel designed to carry human explorers to deep ocean sites

density: the amount of mass in a certain volume of space

electromagnet: a magnet that produces its magnetic field from an electric current in a coil of wire

electromagnetic waves: the back-and-forth pulsing of electricity and magnetism that travels through space. Light is an electromagnetic wave.

galaxy: a system of billions of stars that travel together through space. The Sun is a star in the Milky Way galaxy.

mass: a property of matter that measures its resistance to the change of its motion

matter: a physical substance that has mass and is made of atoms and subatomic particles

nebula: an object in the night sky that has an indefinite or fuzzy appearance. Most nebulas are galaxies.

particle accelerator: a machine that accelerates subatomic particles to extremely high speeds and then produces collisions that may yield undiscovered particles

radioactivity: a phenomenon that takes place within the nucleus of an atom, in which smaller particles are emitted with high energies

remotely operated vehicle (ROV): an undersea exploration vehicle that does not carry passengers and is run by scientists in larger, nearby vessels

rover: a vehicle designed to travel on and explore the surface of another world

space probe: a spacecraft or machine carried by a spacecraft designed to explore another body in the universe

spectrum: the mixture of colors in a light source

Standard Model: the theory describing the basic particles that compose all matter

subatomic particles: particles smaller than the nucleus of an atom

SOURCE NOTES

8   Jacques Yves Cousteau, quoted at BrainyQuote, 2009. http://www.brainyquote
.com/quotes/quotes/j/jacquesyve204406.html (July 1, 2009).

12   Rhian Waller, e-mail message to author, November 12, 2008.

13   Larry Shumaker, quoted in Amy E. Nevala, "Alvin's Pilots," *Oceanus*, June 9, 2009,
http://www.whoi.edu/oceanus/viewArticle.do?id=5599 (July 1, 2009).

20   Edward Norton Lorentz, "Predictability: Does the Flap of a Butterfly's Wings
in Brazil Set Off a Tornado in Texas" (paper presented at the 139th meeting of
the American Association for the Advancement of Science, Washington, DC,
December 29, 1972).

20   Robert Heinlein, *Time Enough for Love* (New York: G. P. Putnam, 1973), 371.

29   Eugene Shoemaker, quoted in Fred Bortz, *To the Young Scientist: Reflections on Doing
and Living Science* (Danbury, CT: Franklin Watts, 1997), 19–20.

30   John F. Kennedy, address before a joint session of the U.S. Congress,
Washington, D.C., May 25, 1961, available online at http://www.jfklibrary.org/
Historical+Resources/Archives/Reference+Desk/ Speeches/JFK/003POF03National
Needs05251961.htm (July 1, 2009).

31   Neil Armstrong, quoted in Apollo 11 Lunar Surface Journal, June 3, 2009,
http://history.nasa.gov/alsj/a11/a11.step.html (August 1, 2009).

31   Craig Nelson, *Rocket Men: The Epic Story of the First Men on the Moon* (New York:
Viking, 2009), 259.

33   Eugene Cernan, *The Last Man on the Moon*, with Don Davis. (New York:
Macmillan, 1999), 337.

40   Michael Griffin, quoted in Benjamin Wallace-Wells, "Mars or Bust," *Rolling Stone*,
February 23, 2006.

48   Jim Bertel, "Hubble Space Telescope's Future Hangs in Balance," *Space Daily*, April
21, 2005, http://www.spacedaily.com/news/hubble-05n.html (July 1, 2009).

53   Stephen W. Hawking, *A Brief History of Time: From the Big Bang to Black Holes* (New
York: Bantam Books, 1988), 8–9.

66–67   Monica Dunford, e-mail message to author, July 2, 2009.

68   Lyndon Evans, "CERN Inaugurates the LHC," CERN, 2008, http://press.web
.cern.ch/press/PressReleases/Releases2008/PR16.08E.html (July 1, 2009).

SELECTED BIBLIOGRAPHY

Bell, Jim. *Postcards from Mars: The First Photographer on the Red Planet*. New York: Dutton, 2006.

Bortz, Fred. *To the Young Scientist: Reflections on Doing and Living Science*. Danbury, CT: Franklin Watts, 1997.

Burrows, William E. *This New Ocean: The Story of the First Space Age*. New York: Random House, 1998.

Cernan, Eugene. *The Last Man on the Moon*. With Don Davis. New York: Macmillan, 1999.

Dyson, Marianne. *Space and Astronomy: Decade by Decade*. New York: Facts on File, 2007.

Flannery, Tim. *The Weather Makers: How Man Is Changing the Climate and What It Means for Life on Earth*. Boston: Atlantic Monthly Press, 2006.

Levy, David H. *Shoemaker by Levy: The Man Who Made an Impact*. Princeton, NJ: Princeton University Press, 2000.

Nelson, Craig. *Rocket Men: The Epic Story of the First Men on the Moon*. New York: Viking, 2009.

Nevala, Amy E. "Building the Next-Generation *Alvin* Submersible: Plan Offers a Roadmap to Extend Sub's Diving Capacity to Reach 99 Percent of the Seafloor." *Oceanus*, November 10, 2008. http://www.whoi.edu/oceanus/viewArticle.do?id=53066 (October 15, 2009).

Robinson, Laura. "The Coral-Climate Connection: The Skeletons of Corals on the Seafloor Preserve Records of How Ocean Circulation Has Changed." *Oceanus*, October 20, 2006. Available online at http://www.whoi.edu/oceanus/viewArticle.do?id=17026 (October 15, 2009).

Watson, Fred. *Stargazer: The Life and Times of the Telescope*. Cambridge, MA: Da Capo, 2005.

Woods Hole Oceanographic Institution. "DSV Alvin: 25 Years of Discovery." *Oceanus*, Winter 1988–1989.

FURTHER READING AND WEBSITES

Books

Bortz, Fred. *Beyond Jupiter: The Story of Planetary Astronomer Heidi Hammel*. Danbury, CT: Franklin Watts, 2005. Be on the scene with Heidi Hammel and other astronomers as the Voyager spacecraft sends back images of Uranus and Neptune. Also share Hammel's discoveries from Hubble Space Telescope images of planetary collisions with pieces of Comet Shoemaker-Levy 9.

——. *The Library of Subatomic Particles*. New York: Rosen, 2004. Follow the explorers of the subatomic world, and discover what their findings mean to science and technology. This six-book set includes *The Electron, The Proton, The Neutron, The Neutrino, The Photon,* and *The Quark*.

Croswell, Ken. *Ten Worlds: Everything That Orbits the Sun.* Rev. ed. Honesdale, PA: Boyds Mills Press, 2006. Striking photos highlight this story of the planets and other bodies in our solar system.

Kuhn, Betsy. *The Race for Space: The United States and the Soviet Union Compete for the New Frontier.* Minneapolis: Twenty-First Century Books, 2007. Feel the excitement of the international competition to put humans on the Moon.

Matsen, Bradford. *The Incredible Submersible Alvin Discovers a Strange Deep-Sea World.* Berkeley Heights, NJ: Enslow, 2003. This book describes one of *Alvin*'s most memorable discoveries—the 1977 dive off the Galápagos Islands.

Silverstein, Alvin, Virginia Silverstein, and Laura Silverstein Nunn. *Global Warming,* Minneapolis: Twenty-First Century Books, 2009. Learn how human activity and the greenhouse effect have changed the climate on Earth.

Websites

Hubble Site

http://hubblesite.org/
The official Hubble website explains the construction, workings, and mission of the HST. The site also contains a gallery of Hubble images (planets, nebulas, stars, and more), an interactive map for locating the HST in orbit, and a section on exploring astronomy.

The Large Hadron Rap on YouTube

http://www.youtube.com/watch?v=j50ZssEojtM
Scientist Kate McAlpine and her colleagues at CERN use rap lyrics to explain the LHC's mission.

NASA Web Site for Students

http://www.nasa.gov/audience/forstudents/index.html
Click the menu link for your grade level to learn about NASA's great work, past, present, and future.

United States Environmental Protection Agency Climate Change Site for Kids

http://epa.gov/climatechange/kids/index.html
Climate change is real, but we can do something about it—if we understand it. This website is a great place to see what scientists know and what they are still trying to find out about the changing climate of our planet.

Woods Hole Oceanographic Institute

http://www.whoi.edu
Click the Education tab and follow the link for "Teaching and Learning" to learn all about oceanography and the many discoveries of the *Alvin* and other research vessels.

INDEX

National Aeronautics and
    Space Administration
    (NASA), 29–30
nebulas, 44
Neptune, 37
neutrinos, 61
neutrons, 60
New Horizons spacecraft, 34, 41
nuclei and atoms, 60

oceans, 8–9, 11. *See also*
    undersea exploration
Opportunity (robotic rover), 40
outer space: the Hubble
    Space Telescope, 43–49;
    interplanetary exploration,
    35–41; lunar exploration
    and, 27–33; mapping the
    universe and, 51–57

particle accelerators: Large
    Hadron Collider (LHC), 64–
    68; matter, 52; subatomic
    particles, 62–64, 70
Pathfinder mission, 39–40
Penzias, Arno, 54–55
Phoenix lander, 41
Pluto, 41
polar ice, 18, 32, 33, 41
precipitation and climate
    change, 23–24
primary cosmic rays, 62
Prospector mission, 32, 33
protons, 60
public policy and climate
    change, 25

quarks, 65, 70

radioactivity, 61
redshifts, 44, 45, 46, 54, 57

remotely operated vehicles
    (ROVs), 9, 11–12, 14, 39–40
rotation of Earth, 20, 21

satellites, 27, 47, 55–56
Saturn, 37
Schmidt, Harrison, 31–32
scuba gear, 8
sea levels, 18, 24
seasons, 20, 21–22
secondary cosmic rays, 62
Shoemaker, Eugene, 27, 28–
    29, 30, 31, 32–33
soil testing and Mars, 38–39,
    41
Sojourner (robotic rover),
    39–40
solar energy, 20, 21–22
Soviet Union, 30, 32, 35
space race, 30
space shuttles, 47
space telescopes, 47–49
spectroscopes, 43
Spirit (robotic rover), 40
Spitzer Space Telescope, 48, 49
Standard Model and subatomic
    particles, 69–70
stars and telescopes, 43
subatomic particles: cosmic rays
    and, 61–62; hadrons and,
    65; Large Hadron Collider
    (LHC) and, 64–68; mass
    and, 69–70; matter and,
    60–61; particle accelerators
    and, 57, 62–64
submarines, 9, 10
Superconducting Super
    Collider (SSC), 65, 66
superconducting wires, 68
supernovas, 56, 57

telescopes, 5, 42, 43–49
temperature: climate change
    and, 23, 24; oceans and,
    11; of planets and moons,
    36, 37, 47; of the universe,
    54, 56
time zero and the big bang,
    52–53
Titanic, 14
titanium, 10, 11
topography and climate
    models, 20, 22

ultraviolet light, 46, 49
undersea exploration, 6, 7–15
United Nations Environmental
    Programme, 25
universe, the: age of, 53;
    expansion of, 45; mapping,
    51–57
Uranus, 37

Venera 1 spacecraft, 35
Venus, 23, 35–36
Viking missions, 38–39
volcanos, 19, 37
Voyager mission, 37

Waller, Rhian, 12, 15
water: on Europa, 37; on Mars,
    40; on the Moon, 32
water pressure, 8–9, 10
wavelengths and light, 46
weather, 17–19, 23–24
white dwarfs, 57
Wilkinson Microwave
    Anisotropy Probe (WMAP),
    50, 56
Wilson, Robert, 54–55
World Meteorological
    Organization, 25

About the Author

Fred Bortz is a scientist and writer of science and technology for young people. In his books, articles, and personal appearances, he shares with his audience the joy of discovery that fueled his previous twenty-five-year career in teaching and research in physics, engineering, and science education. From 1979 through 1994, he was involved in research at Carnegie Mellon University, from which he earned his doctorate in physics in 1971. He is also a regular reviewer of science books for several major metropolitan newspapers.

Photo Acknowledgments

The images in this book are used with the permission of: NASA, ESA, M. Livio and the Hubble Heritage Team (STScI/AURA), p. 5; © Henry Groskinsky/Time & Life Pictures/Getty Images, p. 6; © Publiphoto/Photo Researchers, Inc., p. 7; © Morozova Tatyana/Shutterstock Images, p. 8; Photo by Woods Hole Oceanographic Institution, p. 9; © Bettmann/CORBIS, p. 10; Courtesy of the National Oceanic and Atmospheric Administration Central Library Photo Collection, pp. 11, 12, 13, 73 (bottom left); © Pierre Mion/National Geographic/Getty Images, p. 14 (main); © John Chiasson/National Geographic/Getty Images, p. 14 (inset); photo supplied by Rhian Waller (University of Hawaii) and taken by Dann Blackwood (USGS, Woods Hole), p. 15; © Mike Norton/Shutterstock Images, p. 16; © Galyna Andrushko/Shutterstock Images, p. 17; © Vin Morgan/AFP/Getty Images, p. 18; © Erik S. Lesser/Getty Images, p. 19; © Laura Westlund/Independent Picture Service, pp. 21, 46, 60; © MPI/Stringer/Getty Images, pp. 23, 31; NASA image by Robert Simmon, based on GISS surface temperature analysis data, pp. 24, 73 (top center); © Saeed Khan/AFP/Getty Images, p. 25; NASA, pp. 26, 42, 47, 48, 73 (bottom right); courtesy U.S. Geological Survey, p. 27; © Harvey Lloyd/Taxi/Getty Images, p. 28; © William H. Bond/National Geographic/Getty Images, p. 29; NASA Ames Research Center, p. 32; NASA/JPL, pp. 34, 36, 37, 38; TASS/Sovfoto, p. 35; NASA/JSC/Stanford University, p. 39; © Space Frontiers/Hulton Archive/Getty Images, p. 40; NASA/JPL-Caltech/University of Arizona/Texas A&M University, p. 41; © Jean-Leon Huens/National Geographic/Getty Images, p. 43; © Margaret Bourke-White/Time & Life Pictures/Getty Images, p. 44; NASA/JPL-Caltech/K. Gordon (University of Arizona), p. 49; NASA/WMAP Science Team, p. 50; COBE Project, DMR, NASA, p. 51; © Roger Ressmeyer/CORBIS, p. 54; NASA/COBE Science Team, pp. 55, 73 (top left); MPIA/NASA/Calar Alto Observatory, p. 56; © Dana Berry/CORBIS, p. 57; © Maximilien Brice/CERN, pp. 58, 59, 67, 69; © Mark Garlick/Photo Researchers, p. 61; courtesy of Ernest Orlando Lawrence Berkeley National Laboratory Image Library, p. 63; © AC Team/CERN, p. 64; © Maximilien Brice, Claudia Marcelloni/CERN, p. 71 (top); © Joao Pequenao/CERN, p. 71 (bottom); NASA, ESA, and the Hubble SM4 ERO Team, p. 73 (top right); © Michael Hoch/CERN, p. 73 (right center); NASA/JPL/Cornell University, p. 73 (bottom center).

Front cover: NASA/COBE Science Team (top left); © Michael Hoch/CERN (top center); NASA (top right); NASA/JPL/Cornell University (center); courtesy of the National Oceanic and Atmospheric Administration Central Library Photo Collection (bottom left); NASA image by Robert Simmon, based on GISS surface temperature analysis data (bottom center); NASA, ESA, and the Hubble SM4 ERO Team (bottom right).